"Zaji Cox has given the world the profound gift of reimagining. By rendering reality in fragments, glimpses, lyric reveries, and narrative pulses, she has opened up her own experience—with tremendous generosity and compassion—to illuminate how difference is a place of endlessly generative passion. This book is a poetic love song as big as the cosmos. This book brings me back to life."

—**Lidia Yuknavitch**, author of *Thrust*

"*Plums for Months* is a stunning and poetic feat by a true artist. Zaji's ability to skillfully fill brevity with depth and hang light over the unknown while smoothing the sharp edges of life with enchantment, all through the wonders of a child's mind, is inexplicably brilliant."

—**Kesha Ajose-Fisher**, author of *No God Like the Mother*

"*Plums for Months* is one of the most beautiful books I have ever read, or held, and one which defies every category. It leaves me not knowing what to call it so I'll just call it MAGIC."

—**Jennifer Pastiloff**, author of *On Being Human*

"While every neurodiverse person is unique, it is in the relatable observations and unique worldview that Zaji Cox's vignettes shine. An amalgamate anthem, *Plums for Months* shows how to seek solitude, coping, and comfort in everyday interactions."

—**Joe Biel**, author of *Good Trouble:*
Building a Successful Life & Business with Autism

Plums for Months

PLUMS
FOR
MONTHS

memories of a wonder-filled,
neurodivergent childhood

ZAJI COX

FOREST AVENUE PRESS
Portland, Oregon

Library of Congress Cataloging-in-Publication Data

Names: Cox, Zaji, 1994- author.
Title: Plums for months : memories of a wonder-filled, neurodivergent childhood / Zaji Cox.
Description: Portland : Forest Avenue Press, 2023. | Summary: "As a neurodivergent child in a hundred-year-old house, Zaji Cox collects grammar books, second-hand toys, and sightings of feral cats. She dances and cartwheels through self-discovery and doubt, guided by her big sister and their devoted single mother. Through short essays that evoke the abundant imagination of childhood, Plums for Months explores the challenges of growing up mixed race and low-income on the outskirts of Portland, Oregon"-- Provided by publisher.
Identifiers: LCCN 2022044373 | ISBN 9781942436539 (paperback) | ISBN 9781942436546 (ebook)
Subjects: LCSH: Cox, Zaji, 1994- | Autistic people--Biography. | Racially mixed people--Biography. | Neurodiversity.
Classification: LCC HV1570.22.C69 A3 2023 | DDC 616.85/8820092 [B]--dc23/eng/20220926
LC record available at https://lccn.loc.gov/2022044373

"How Old" was first published in Portland Metrozine

Distributed by Publishers Group West

Published in the United States of America
by Forest Avenue Press LLC
Portland, Oregon

Printed in the United States

Forest Avenue Press LLC
P.O. Box 80134
Portland, OR 97280
forestavenuepress.com

1 2 3 4 5 6 7 8 9

To Mom,
Bevin,
Guardadian,
and the cats.

One Toy

IT'S SOME KIND OF wolf-hawk biped, brown-gray with an aggressive V of anger, or maybe strength, on its brow. Free from box, sticker, or tags, it lies in a weathered and bent blue bin, crowded between worn baby dolls and zoo animals, under bent Polly Pockets and silent T-rexes with roars long gone. I spotted it under the plastics and fabrics, weaving through the musty smell of former homes and hands and sliding my fingers upon the toy, dull and scratched but weird and wonderful. I push aside Barbie in her stained pink-and-white dress to hold the plastic creature up to my face, feeling a thrill at the sharpness of its canines, the unforgiving jut of its jaw, its razor feathers curved over giant clawed feet. Its deep brown eyes are the exact same shade as mine, and they scream *power*. My want for anything in the world has never matched my want for this right now. I turn pleading and urgent eyes to my mother. We put back one thing in our basket—a pair of shoes I could do without for now—and I clutch the creature a happy girl. Stained-dress Barbie is left in the bin with her arm half-raised, and I almost wave back.

Braids

MY MOTHER'S FINGERS WEAVE expertly as they form my hair
into braids, one over two under three under one, pale and slender
tangled in dark and thick. "So different from your sister's." A spray
of rosewater, a glide through with the fine-tooth comb.

I think with envy how my sister's is longer, though she has
almost nine years on me to have the extra inches. I think of how
hers is like mine yet unlike mine from roots to ends. How the hair
of her father and our mother gives it a coarseness different from
the thickness of mine.

Sometimes I'm asked if I have an afro if my hair isn't in braids,
and I have to explain to confused faces that it's just … *poofy*.
The faces never completely understand, just melt into a slightly
less-confused expression. Sometimes the eyes will bulge and then
squint and the person will say, *Interesting*, looking at me like I'm
an exotic animal.

"COULD YOU PLEASE MAKE them as small and thin as you can
this time?"

It's the only way they'll move fluidly like straight hair. Like
the girls in adventure movies, whose ponytails flutter behind

them as they dash through forests and mountain paths, or the girls in Christmas movies who meet Santa and turn their heads in glee, pigtails swinging and brushing their shoulders. I want pigtails that swing like they do in movies, and so I ask my mom every time to make the braids as tiny as she can. Because if they're too big, they will be stiff and hardly move at all. They will look ridiculous.

I HAVE A VISION like a movie scene: I'm leaning back in a chair like the one I'm in now upstairs. My braids are falling over the back and I am shaking my head while I talk about something. What I'm talking about isn't important, nor is the situation, really. But what is important are the braids, mingling together so well you'd think they were another mass of straight, dark, perfect hair.

SHE TELLS ME, "I'M making them as tight and tiny as I can," and I know she is. Because she knows why, even though I never say it. And when she's done I am so grateful for her and her expert fingers, because the braids do indeed move. They've grown just enough that they move more each time. Though they are weighed down with moisture and product, but still.

My sister sees when I get downstairs and she runs her hand through my braids, her own hair in a cascade of extensions that fall down her back. She marvels at how long my hair's getting. A thrill swells inside, washing over my outside to make me beautiful.

The thrill saturates the bite of melancholy at the thought that my hair could not have turned out like our mom's, a silky sway dyed red by henna that glides past her shoulders. I keep the bite sleeping in its home, safely blanketed and tucked away, as I move my head to make my braids dangle.

A New Almost-Home

THE FIR AND CEDAR trees over Palmblad Road are towers under which a mother and two daughters drive to the house whose weight is rooted in the ground. Gravel shuffles under car tires and the doors click and creak open to a world of cool, moist air. The trio emerges to marvel under a gray sky so unlike the clear, hot desert air they left behind. The home, owned by the mother's father, stands waiting.

Through the months that flow into years, the mother and daughters make a home of the weathered hundred-and-ten-year-old house that shelters mice and spiders among the two acres of property that are not theirs. Over time, objects accumulate in rooms to make the house feel like it belongs to the three. College textbooks, family pictures, and framed artwork brought by the mother lean on downstairs shelves. In the mother's bedroom, picture books for the younger daughter lie on one side of the bed and long, text-heavy books for the mother lie on the other. The older daughter's room holds incense, CDs, magazine photos, and historical fiction novels. The younger daughter's room is decorated with toys and a rainbow of clothing in the nook of a closet; books soon start to pile on one another. Her wolf-bird Transformer eventually finds its spot in the plastic-toy container under the bed. Its legs don't fold in the way they should, but she sort of likes that this makes it unlike any other.

As the rain of autumn becomes the rain of winter, the mother and older daughter keep the house warm with chopped firewood and the downstairs heater that sometimes works. Summer finally arrives to bring enough blackberries, blueberries, grapes, apples, and plums for months. Hands scrape past thorns and reach above tall branches to pick the very best fruits to cook with. The younger daughter helps cut back the invasion of blackberry bushes around the sides of the house, whose vines tap the windows; her small hands curl around hedge clippers and reach as close to the roots as possible. With nimble fingers, she helps mend the broken downstairs window with plastic and tape.

Some nights the three listen to the wind howl, the house creak, or the rain and wet tree branches thrum against the house, and continue to adjust to the new nature. They huddle closer in the living room, closer to their popcorn and movie and each other, and let the outside music play in the background.

A Saturday

A NAME SCRATCHED ONTO white paper with a seagull-feather pen found in the tall wild grasses filled with blackberry ink; seeds picked out of a fallen husk, planted in the front yard soil, and watered with spit; sticks bent and ruler-straight combined with leaves damp and crackling-dry, assembled with wildflowers to make tiny homes for tiny creatures; branches under a towering cedar tree shoved aside to make an entrance to a hiding place that provides cover from the rain and room to jump; wood brought in to help build a fire, whose dance draws the eyelids lower.

Watching My Sister
Chop Firewood

thunk

A fold of flannel and fleece.

thunk

The soft grinding of earth under hiking boots by the tree stump.

thunk

Gloved hands wrapped around a weathered axhandle.

thunk

Braided hair falling free of its bun, hanging around ears and face.

thunk

The shock of pale inside the log after

thunk

each enlarging split.

thunk

Wood scent intermingled with the moistness of rain.

thunk-
crack

The clatter of the log on the white wire basket pile;

the reach of a muscled arm for another to

thunk.

Congregation

MY CONFIRMATION OF A fairy-tale life comes the day we interrupt a black-cat meeting.

The mundanity of a return trip from the grocery store dissolves in the midst of this mystical feline presence. They sit like little ink spots at the end of our gravel driveway as the three of us roll up in the car, and we fall into a hush as if under a spell. Some latecomers are strolling in, and they all face each other, calm and pacing, all swiveling heads and flicking tails. There are at least ten. I have never seen so many cats in one place before.

This land—the property owned not by us but our mom's dad, with this hundred-and-ten-year-old house, the land that we have made into our home—suddenly feels like it belongs to another. Someone not human. Our mom slows the car. We three watch from afar, trying desperately to preserve this moment. Time vanishes.

The black cats could be talking about anything, sinewy in their motions and slow-blinking as they look at one another. Subtle yet confident. My mom and sister whisper from the front of the car while my reverence multiplies.

I find that I am holding my breath, worried about the inevitable grand moment when one sees us and alerts the others. A shock, a jump, an urgent scatter. I will my mother and sister not to make a noise.

And yet, slowly, they begin to disperse one by one. As if planned. I slowly let out my breath, and my muscles relax. *Don't go.*

They almost seem reluctant to leave. I imagine them planning their next meeting.

Our only evidence is our word.

Jerry

My CURLY-TAILED COMPANION, ALWAYS ready to talk.

I came up with the name on the day I met him and his brother, riding home from Fred Meyer, where our mom's coworker friend had transferred their cardboard cat carriers over to us in a back room of the store. He is named after Jerry the mouse, because I liked that name better than Tom, and it just felt friendlier to me. Very fitting, as it turned out. The tail curls not like a question mark but like a smile, matching his persistent mood.

Neo is his brother, named and chosen by my big sister. He is sleek and moody, happy when you pet him just right. Named after the *Matrix* guy. He looks like he ought to be constantly wearing sunglasses.

Jerry and Neo recognize our intentions and adjust to our individual energies, each of them spending more time with each of us.

I soon find in Jerry a listener. He is there when I can't communicate right with the human world to which I supposedly belong. He sits with me in front of the downstairs heater that sometimes works while I read for hours, a friend in silence when all I want is silence without weight. An absence of judgement punctuated by a rumbling purr. A listener who is always at home waiting for me. Appearing whenever I need to talk but not talk, with his curly-smile tail.

The Cats Outside

THE CATS WE SEEM to attract to our land are all black except for one.

While we jump on our trampoline, with its deteriorating ring of blue plastic, the duo hear us and approach. She is sleek, the gray of a fall noon sky, with eyes deep-ice blue. He is black as obsidian, as midnight, as the unexplored sea, with autumn-leaf eyes. We conclude they must be brother and sister.

My sister and I have different names for them. Hers are Ashurbanipal for the black one and Tiglath-Pileser III for his sister.

I choose Abercrombie and Fitch.

Over time the gray one comes less and less as we jump on the trampoline or play badminton or swing on the tire swing. Eventually it is just Ash/Abby who comes to see us. We do not know why Tiglath/Fitch has stopped coming, but we miss her beautiful gray rippling pelt. But Ash/Abby stands on shoulders and goes *ah!* instead of *meow*. He rises onto his hind legs when rubbing his head on a hand. And he can jump all the way from the ground to your chest to be held.

Jerry and Neo inside become jealous. The outside cats are a bonded pair, different as they are; watching from the other side of the dining room window, I think our two can see the bond edging toward us.

When we finally return inside, Jerry and Neo's affection doubles. We belong to them.

Hunter

THERE WAS ANOTHER WHO came before our cat friends, on thick dark paws from the tangle of grasses.

He was the first feral cat. Also black. Also from the unmown wild.

Hunter walked on steps weighted with Earth connection, each one leaving behind a note that resounded lower and deeper than most cats. He watched us from the tall grasses. He came when he felt like it. His fur was matted in patches, rough-smooth and missing in places.

Needle claws. A chipped front fang. Blinks slow and content by a waiting hand. He carried the aura of one who was there long before us and from a family who was there long before us. From a line extending perhaps even before the house itself.

When he was gone, his footstep-note lingered from the deep grasses and everywhere he had walked, so low and present that he wasn't really gone.

Dusk Creatures

ONE DISTANT BARK BECOMES two, two become ten and ten become countless. As the sun sinks lower, I let the outside pack of dogs of the Gresham house howl me to sleep.

On abundant summer nights after bike rides down the Springwater Corridor Trail, ice-cream-truck treats, and sprinkler games, I watch bat silhouettes against the sky and think about school.

When I sleep over at Daddy's in his faraway Portland home that always looks and smells new, the dogs are replaced by distant frogs—millions, it seems—who croak their nonstop songs through the night among a backdrop of green. I think about the dogs singing the song of the old creaking house.

The night before my first-ever gymnastics meet, floor and beam choreography run through my head in sync with the voices of the dogs. Anxious speculations of the unknown shoot up and around me like a jagged chorus.

I never see the dogs except in my mind, dozens of ruffled pelts and raised snouts, grays and browns blending into a wild mass together and into the field beyond. Voices nonthreatening but insistent: reminders of who claims what.

Old Photo

I HOLD THE EDGES of the little rectangle gingerly, sliding it out of the frame that rests on my dresser at Daddy's house. Here in Portland, Zaji's room is white, with toys in their own shining gold chest. Books are lined up neatly, though there aren't as many of them, and *Archie* comics hide in the sliding-door closet. The bigger window shows not a wild forest yard but a cul-de-sac, with straight white houses like this one. A neat and paved nature trail cuts through the grass and trees off to the side. Instead of classic rock, I hear smooth jazz floating up the stairs.

I am careful not to smudge the shiny side of the photo. Three-year-old me remains pristine, a perfect blur in pink and white suspended from the monkey bars. I lift it to my face and smell the print of ink on paper. Each color has its own scent. The bitterness of the corner shadow made by a finger covering the lens; the almost-sweet pink ink of the pants over my straightened legs.

My eyes are drawn toward the steady grip on the bars, the knees and feet pressed together, the little frown of concentration.

This world in the photo is tan and brown, with sides of adobe buildings and flat desert land. I can hear the quiet of the New Mexico desert, my first home. It's not like the quiet of the green, which speaks of birds and dampness, soft patches of moss nestled between towers of trees. The desert's quiet is a flat and open, all-encompassing dryness, wind hushing between dry brush and tumbleweeds. No forest shades the background. What green there is stands tall and brave under the relentless sun. I think of Daddy's side of the family there, sunny and smiling.

Coming-Home Smell

IT'S ALWAYS THE SMELL of cigarette smoke—never hers, she doesn't smoke—that comes home with her when she leans down to kiss me as I lay in bed under the yellow painted stars on my pink walls, bringing stories along with it. Most of the time I pull away from small touches—my sensory irritation—but I can lie still under the weighted blanket of relief at her safe return. I am finally able to relax, the bitter scent intertwining with perfume that smells like the color of amber, creating the scent of mothers who look for someone who can keep up with them, mothers returned from somewhere foreign and grown-up.

I wonder who she's met tonight in the mystery of strangers.

I pretend to be asleep, if only to bask in the gentle saturation of comfort. I pretend to be asleep if only to feel kisses and strands of hair brush my face. My worry is always on overdrive at thoughts of nighttime driving and dark, dense grown-up places to meet other grown-ups, and I pretend to be asleep with the sound of keys and loud front-door creak in my mind. Images of her strong gaze rising above that of others weave together in my mind, and I pretend to be asleep if only to feel the warmth of mother body heat above me, a gentle hand tucking me in to tell me she is home safe.

Streams

IT'S A LONG DRIVE from Gresham to Portland, passing by other old houses tucked behind overgrown front yards and snaking past strip malls and restaurants, Goodwills and grocery stores, past stretches of empty lots filled with tall grasses I want to run through, past the turn that takes us to Daddy's house, then bumping over the Blue Line MAX train tracks and down the portal of I-84.

Then, buildings grow in height and streets get denser with cars and people. Downtown Portland is flannel and denim, business suits and click-clacking heels breezing by patched-vest wearers with collarless dogs; it is college students in that confusing age between teenager and parent-age emerging from vegan and vegetarian restaurants we *wish* they had in Gresham. My sense of wonder expands. Everything's faster, denser, *more*.

We as a family dip into lives, from one into another like they're little streams. One visit brings us to the life of dark colors and spiked hair, loud concert music and legs-getting-tired standing on sticky floors; of tall people in heavy black boots, of dancing that turns into movements that look frightening until my mom smiles and shakes her head at the shoving bodies; of my uncle's bandmates who smile warmly at my shy averted eyes. I want so badly to ask them how they can possibly get on a stage before countless others and become such loose, larger versions of themselves. The words build inside me and I cannot get them out, but they seem to understand.

It is rare that we come for these special downtown visits, into the pockets of life to be found in corners and blocks, buildings and towers. It takes all I have not to ask for us to come down again and again, night after night.

Weeks later, our next visit brings us to another life, one of gentler music, strings and choral voices a steady flow above our heads; plush velvet seats like the velvet of my dress; hot chocolate warm between my palms as we watch leaps and turns in pointe shoe shimmer, tulle, and tiaras. This life is the utter onstage magic of a growing Christmas tree, falling snow, and whole moving set pieces. It's not long before I begin to imagine myself standing up there before the crowd. Expressing the swell of emotion that I feel when I hear music and see motion in my mind's eye.

But the idea of eyes, so many pairs all on me, brings me back within the mass of people.

We wade expertly between the worlds made of electric guitar under strobe lights and arabesques among gingerbread and candy canes. Both carry an aliveness enough to make my breath catch.

Downtown winks at us as we head back through the I-84 portal. A transformation occurs, and here are the familiar shadows of the trees—our trees—hugging us into time that moves differently.

Into our unhurried river of a life under the stars.

In my bedroom I pull my Powerpuff Girls pajamas from the closet and replace my scuffed black shoes and dark coat, or my tights and hand-me-down dress, with clothing loose and worn. Jerry jumps onto the bed with me as I lay back and think about the swift streams of downtown. The difference of the stages. They stick with me, opposites that flow together and apart, like a dampness that won't dry.

How Many More Times?

MEASURED STEPS IN RHYTHM with the screen, VHS playing Britney Spears coming down an elaborate spiral staircase; I am responsible for making sure her steps and my sister's are the same. Make sure their struts are identical. Watch closely from the living room couch audience.

When can I go to sleep?

My sister's vibrato must begin on exactly the right count, not a millisecond too late. She has to hit the low low note in *I can't get no sat-is-fac-tion*, but not like she's trying to do so, and again, has to time it just right.

When will Mom come home?

Hair long and blond swishes under its hat and across the back as one runs back and forth across the giant stage. Hair dark brown and coiled in a bun stays tight in its place as the other runs back and forth across the creaking wood tiles under the overhead light.

Is this the last time for real now?

But even as eyes close and ears strain to hear for the sound of a car in the driveway, even with the thoughts of a soft bed upstairs, they mix with thoughts of how a sister in a late-night living room does it so much better than Britney, the best of any performer seen before, with furiously perfect moves and a flawless voice that bursts past old walls. How she simply needs a real stage like the one on the screen and not more practice. But that's just how she is.

Neighbors

NEXT DOOR—TO THE right if you're standing in the yard with the house to your back—separated by hedges and blackberry bushes, we have llamas for neighbors. We think they are the funniest things, with their tightly curled pelts and squinty eyes. You can see them if you go past our tall barrier of cedars to the wilder part of the property, where the blueberry bushes, grapevine, and dilapidated shed are. Past the line strung between two poles that's just low enough for me to help hang clothes on summer days. Here, there aren't any hedges and you can see them peering above the blackberry bushes.

To the left is a woman and her husband in a house about as old as ours. The woman, who is eighty-something, gets up on her roof very early every morning to work on it. She has no animals in her yard, but she thinks the outdoor cats are sweet. I'm a little jealous to discover that they visit her too.

The day I realize the llamas aren't gentle giants like horses, I start to like them a little less. I edge my little-kid hand near the fence palm-up, but they are standoffish and uninterested. At first I don't believe my sister when she tells me that they spit when they don't like you, but then I see them do it to no one in particular and actually think it is kind of silly. Despite the fact that I don't try to pet them anymore, it makes me angry that the fence surrounding them is spiked and possibly electric.

The neighbor to the left hasn't got a fence with spikes, but what she does have are berries and things to be picked in her backyard like ours. We begin to visit her more and more because she just has too much for herself and her husband.

My sister practices for performances diligently at home; on nice days she goes outside to lightly work on her finger cymbals skills for belly dance or drumming with a blanket stuffed inside to muffle the noise. One day when she is drumming, the neighbors to the right turn up their country music very loud, so loud that she has to come inside to hear herself practice.

Sometimes we help our neighbor to the left with yard work. She doesn't really need the help, but in return she gives us some of the pies she makes with the fruits of her yard. We see her much more often than the neighbors to the right.

I think about how sometimes neighbors, with their llamas or bucketfuls of berries or country music or early rising, will be there for you. In their own ways. Separated by fence or by choice, they will be there, ready to either drown out or welcome with open arms the selves that you provide.

Styled

So ANGRY AT IT for the pain on my head and the burning in my arms and not conforming to the brush the way I want.

So angry at it and how it can only be one way or something is wrong with me and I am misshapen.

So angry at it that it's the first thing I as a child associate with the word *hopeless*.

So angry at it that the only thing keeping the wide-tooth comb from breaking in my hands is the fact that this is the only one we have to help tame it.

So angry at it that there is a day I decide to suspend my care and let it free and bask in the gaping and laughing because *it's okay and I'm laughing too*.

So angry because I want to love it, but its tangles and thickness make it too difficult.

Confrontation

MIXED WITH BLACK, THE deep evening blue frames the down-the-street neighbor's driveway, his army-green truck shining as it reflects the streetlight. Leaves arch over our heads as my sister and I wait in the car, watching our mom's steps strong with *my daughter* go up to the man's door. Too far to hear, we see the calm inside her work to guide and tame the anger, tame the *my daughter* to a volume that won't shake the trees with the white noise of woman-yell. I award her one thousand points, and our neighbor negative one thousand. In the fading light I can barely see him, a figure standing tall in his doorway. I imagine what it must have looked like earlier, him yelling at my sister on her solo walk while she listened to her Walkman, accusing her and her "friends" of breaking into his truck while he was at work. He accused her of stealing CDs.

I can see his truck from where I sit in the backseat. None of the windows are broken like he said my sister and these phantom friends of hers had done. I subtract another thousand points from him. I almost laughed when she came home and told us about it— not at what happened but at the absurdity of my responsible sister doing something like that.

What We Are

IN THE TWO OF us we are many: Irish, Danish, French, German, Native American, Black, white, and more that we don't know, buried in history like our Native ancestor who was kidnapped from her tribe. So when my sister tells me about all the people who squint at her and ask what *is* she, or my classmate draws a picture of me and her in class and I am colored the darkest, chocolate brown, I want to hold out my arm, my sister's arm, and peel back every layer to show the white, the Black, the Native American, the German, the French, the Danish, the Irish, the many.

A Stage

I MAKE A STAGE of the springboard floor at the gym.

Compulsory-level gymnastics routines are all the same, to the same music if done on floor, with no personalization in choreography until you reach optional levels.

Precise, exact, and structured, doing the same routines multiple times a week allows me to add personal flourish to the dance elements on floor and beam. Settling into the familiar, I stretch my open hand and swish it through the air; I engage my quadriceps and outer rotators to lift my hyperextended leg close to my shoulder and hold it there as long as I can. My first position right before starting a floor routine is so turned out I look like a ballet dancer; my leaps extend to a full split midair. The bright lights of the gym and the echo of multiple voices become background noise when I focus. I blush when teammates and coaches compliment my grace, while inside I am smiling twice as wide as I allow on my face.

Three days a week for four hours a day I am at the gym, jogging and conditioning and practicing skills. Settling my brain into planned-out moves. Practice even follows me home: my sister works at my gym and eventually becomes my coach. Like a map the motions are laid out in front of me to follow, and I focus on where I must improve—smoothing the connection between the leap and step forward on beam, not stuttering my last few steps in my sprint toward the vault springboard; engaging my leg's fast-twitch muscles to push quick in the transition from low bar to high bar. When we get to competition season, I get before the judges and reach for a score close to ten.

Repetition. Structure. Routine.

Nowadays, optional levels start at seven. In order to climb my way there, when I can finally, *finally*, dance and tumble to the music I want, I need to master the moves I don't have yet. The front tuck on floor, back walkover on beam, or flyaway dismount on bars make my throat constrict in apprehension. The moves where I can't fully see where I'm going. The thought of going alone without a sister-coach to spot me creates mental blocks, which make a brick wall high enough to obscure the map. It makes me dizzy. I watch my teammates and the kids in optional levels punch the floor without hesitation or fear.

I sometimes daydream about the choreography and music of what my own floor routine would look like. But the path to the kind of dance I want is strewn with jagged rocks and barriers, and there are times when level seven feels impossible.

So, in the meantime, I fashion a temporary stage on the blue carpet of the gym's springboard floor with my compulsory-level routine and think about ways to destroy a brick wall.

The Five Senses

THE WOODEN FOLDOUT DESK wobbles in front of our big downstairs TV as I set down my favorite meal of all meals ever—beans, rice, and cheese in our chipped pink happy-face bowl—next to my homework. An episode of *The Fairly OddParents* I've seen dozens of times plays in the background as I hold my purple pencil poised over the handout. Empty rectangular boxes hold the words *sight, smell, sound, touch,* and *taste* with simple images of corresponding body parts underneath. I have yet to see images on a homework handout like this with a nose drawing shaped like mine—not pointed but flatter like my dad's. Though mine curves up a little at the end, so maybe I never will see one like it.

For *sight,* I want to write about the paintings I see in my head when I listen to my favorite songs. How the swirls of burgundy and deep brown move slowly and fluidly around each other, accented by halos of gold.

For *smell,* I want to write about the way it folds into taste when you inhale the scents of lilacs and roses. How light-colored ones smell different than dark-colored ones, and how each becomes its own color.

For *sound*, I want to describe the way it floats from my ears to my eyes and can be more than one thing. I want to mention the shivers it gives me when certain notes in music come together just right, or how its absence leaves me with another kind of sound no one else in the world can hear, the soft eternal ringing bells that some call *tinnitus*.

For *touch*, I want to write about the thrill of feeling something pristine and brand-new. A notebook opened for the first time after school-supply shopping, some pages still stuck together; a slick new DVD in its case that opens with a squeak and click; Polly Pocket dolls and playset unbound from their packaging, so shiny you almost don't want to smudge them with your fingerprints.

And for *taste*, I want to write about this bowl of beans, rice, and cheese. Because it is *so good*, the way the cheese just melts over the pinto beans and brown rice and makes you think of all Mexican food ever because it's the base of everything and fills you up in delicious bites.

There is not enough room in these rectangular boxes to get all of this down. And I'm not quite sure how to get it into words that people will understand; I have a feeling my senses work differently than others' do. I lift my eyes and watch the erratic movements of the characters on the screen, recalling the examples we were given in class—simple things like *books, singing, apples*.

I write down *cartoons, classical music, lilacs*, and *toys*.

For *taste,* however, I keep what I said about beans, rice, and cheese, smushing my words a little smaller near the end to fit inside the box. That one's too good to leave out.

Boys

I DON'T DAYDREAM OF kissing crushes underneath the play structure or cuddling in the back of the school bus. I don't imagine what it would be like to hold hands on the swings or pass heart-shaped notes to them or what the thought of every smile and eventual hug carrying me on a cloud on the way home would feel like. I daydream instead of rescuing them, pulling them aboard my play-structure ship from a grisly fate in a hot-lava sea; I daydream about the school bus ride home going awry one day and getting lost with them in a strange new land, drawn together by the journey back through the unknown. I imagine what would happen if all adults vanished from the earth and our fourth-grade class must endeavor to find them—of course, my crush and I would work together closely, solving the problem with our circle of friends. I share these imaginings with my best friend, and she nods vigorously, her braids like mine shaking around her head as she says "Yes!" to everything. I do this with each of my crushes and we go on all sorts of adventures.

Eventually, however, one of them gets lost during the journey. He either is eaten by a lava shark or becomes lost in the dark and tangled woods. It's because I realize after a while that, despite his spiky blond hair and admirable athleticism, he is actually kind of a jerk during class, with an ever-expanding fourth-grade sports ego. So I decide I don't like him anymore. My best friend agrees.

And so we leave him behind in the woods.

The Scholastic Book Fair

THERE ARE WORLDS AT my fingers:

Jungle adventures, *Undercover Girl* spy kits, puzzles, photo collections of the unseen earth, how-to-draw my favorite cartoon characters, game packs, and next installations in my favorite series. Colors and covers on stands; tables a maze as I walk. Outer jackets so pristine I make myself hold the inner pages only. The smells of the worlds, the weight, the sound of paper sliding on paper. My need for them is too much and it builds to overwhelm my head. My classmates circle the library, its own world an old and dulled backdrop to the temporary rainbow. They furiously flip pages, reach and grab and reach and grab. Their arms ache from fullness. My arms ache from wanting.

I imagine these slick new covers stacked high in my room, separated neatly into to-read, already read, and reread piles. Enough to separate into different genres, as I have already begun to do with what I have. The stacks would grow on the dark brown shelves in my room and I would look at them lovingly from my bed as they created small, neat towers. Like always, I push away the question of how this is fair with the more urgent question of how to decide. I can get only two. The worlds are disappearing.

But then I think: there is one way. There is one way we can afford not only two but them all. I will pay with need. This need and desire for stories and adventure. I will pull it out of my chest and measure it in weight, turn it into currency so I can have them all.

The Girls at Goodwill

I'M STANDING AT THE clothing rack and trying to decide between the blue shirt with frilled sleeves or the one with a dog declaring she's a "diamond in the ruff" when they appear, pushing aside the other shirts and as a result pushing aside the ones I'd had in front of me. But I tend to be kind of unnoticeable at times, so I just step aside to where my frilled-sleeve and cartoon-dog shirts are now. The two girls are wrapped up in their flurry of activity anyway, the two of them more like ten of them. A new-looking watch peeks out from between the secondhand fabric as they sift and debate on which tops go best with their "totally vintage" and "so-ugly-they-aren't-ugly" jeans from the other rack. They talk so much at a certain pitch that I kind of want to curl up and whine. They're acting like people who aren't much older than me, like teenagers, and yet they look the same age as the people who are in my sister's community college classes.

I don't know what to think of them and so I watch the short woman I see shopping here sometimes come over, giving the girls—women?—one look and then shaking her head, in a sort of tired way. Her hand flies through the fabric as she looks for what she wants and makes a selection, muttering something in Spanish to her three kids as they walk away. A teenager with braid extensions like my sister passes by and snickers at the two. They look up briefly, as if to say, *Was that a ghost?* then go back to finding a shirt. They narrow it down to two shirts: one with frilled sleeves like mine has a look that is "bohemian" while another with rhinestones is a little too "gangsta."

I am hoping they will not take as long as it is taking me to decide.

The girl with the watch shrugs. "Both?" And suddenly, with what is apparently the "easiest choice," they are gone. I love their scent as they walk by—I think it's Sea Breeze, that Bath & Body Works perfume I always like to smell during one of our rare mall trips.

There is a familiar twinge as I leave behind the blue frilled sleeves and head back to wherever my mom is by the clearance rack.

The First Week

SIXTH GRADE IS WEIRD.

It's like high school-in-training. I feel like there's a step I missed between fifth grade and sixth, a bridge I overlooked when crossing a too-wide gap. Summer's visit to the squat brick building that is Dexter McCarty Middle School introduced me to a world of winding hallways that go on and on through an interior of dull colors and straight lines. Every so often the school mascot would appear in the cartoonish image of an angry-looking hornet with its fists curled ready to fight. When we stepped through the double doors we were greeted by a group of kids in the cafeteria-gym, uniformed in forest-green-and-black gym clothes as they shouted out a letter of the mascot each time they did a jumping jack. Watching a circle of classmates jogging around them in a swarm, I blinked and wondered if we had stumbled into the wrong place. Surely I was not headed here at only eleven?

My closest elementary-school friends, who live in other districts, will be going elsewhere. My best friend with braids like me will be going to the school that's on the other side of town. So I will be going at the new experience alone. We vow to see each other as often as we can, call and visit each other. But I am still not sure how to handle it, or really how to feel about it, and so I observe and analyze. Look at facts and plan ahead.

One thing I look forward to, though, is the prospect of lockers. Lockers—which signify the ultimate school experience, where you keep all your books and protractors and planners, which you see on every TV show about every school experience—will be here. Every time we drove past Dexter McCarty in the summer, I tried to glance inside to see if we'd have lockers. I thought about a character in one of my favorite book series when she finally made it to sixth grade and hoped my life would be similarly filled with new friends, shiny hallways, art classes, and real textbooks to put in those lockers.

I am ecstatic when I get mine. The only thing is that they slam louder than I'd like. A sound too sharp and unpredictable. But that's okay because my locker partner is nice. In fact, many kids are nice to me, despite my quiet nature and difficulty with inside jokes or most things nonverbal. Even the popular seventh-graders smile real smiles when I glance at them in their matching tube top, lip-glossed, neon bracelet-wearing groups, and say kind things when asking about my gymnastics. (I realize only later that part of this might be due to the fact that my mom works here during the summer.)

So perhaps I don't need to worry about finding new friends to make it through the strangeness of this place, or the self-direction of being on time in a different room before the bell. Perhaps I don't need to worry about trying to match everyone's abrasive jokes, or the sensory overload of bright lights bouncing off gray floor tiles combining with shouts and slamming metal. Perhaps I don't need to worry about hearing talk of real boyfriends and girlfriends, teachers who seem tired of their jobs, or the whole experience so far feeling like the awkward fit of a left shoe on the right foot.

For now it seems to be okay.

Competition

GRIPS PLACED JUST RIGHT, holes around index and ring fingers and dowel situated near the palm. Velcro wrapped around the wristbands, just tight enough but not too tight. Get your chalk from the pile in the container and rub your hands together for just the right amount. Stand ready. Your teammates and sister-coach are watching from the sides, eager: they can rely on you for a good bar score. Watch the judge. You don't need to be reminded not to fidget; being the uneven bars, it's one of the rare times you don't. Watch for his hand to lift and for him to say your name (correctly!) and a good-luck wish. Raise your arms to present and step up to the mat. Face the bars.

Bend the knees and swing the arms back to get a fluid motion as you jump to the low bar and begin the routine ingrained in your body. Engage the lats, traps, dorsi, abs for the kip, let the momentum rotate you around the bar, feel it rest against your hip, then cast to raise your body above and then to stand on the bar. Jump to high bar, engage the biceps and deltoids to bring yourself up, glide in a smooth rhythm while you circle your body around again.

This one … it's one of your best executions.

There is a hush: the area around you, including the crowd of parents, has gone quiet. You feel dozens of eyes on you, which has never happened before. The judges out of the corner of your vision are scribbling furiously while they keep their gaze trained on you, but don't get distracted. And as you feel the dozens of eyes on you and swing on high bar preparing to release from the routine you are somehow executing so well, the familiar routine that today feels so unfamiliar, notice the astounded hush inside you matching that of the crowd that may have uncovered a different you, hidden.

After the slap of your feet on the blue mat when you dismount—always over so quickly, under a minute—there is something like a breath before your team applauds. And the crowd. Like an audience. They keep clapping after you raise your arms to the judges again in the finishing salute and then go to sit down.

Your score is a 9.825. The closest to a ten you've ever gotten.

Your shoulders, which you didn't even realize had been tense, relax. This different, unhidden you basks in the congratulating, the pleasure of pleasing your sister, and the sense of security in your teammates. She wants to go hiding again—but that's okay because you know where she lives and will find her again.

Asperger's Syndrome
what my teacher called it

THAT NAME ONCE GIVEN to a form of autism spectrum disorder in which a person has specific and often obsessive interests, such as memorizing grammar books, and who may experience difficulty relating to other people in social situations.

That term for individuals who fixate on particular interests such as recreating movie soundtrack themes from memory through piano or voice with absolute pitch; that term for those who relate to others differently than the norm.

That label for those who, though experiencing occasional sensory overwhelm/difficulty relating to others or understanding of the nuances of nonverbal communication, focus heavily on tasks such as self-study and story writing and figure out the nuances of connecting with animals/family pets.

That simple label, ever-changing and ever-evolving, for minds with different wiring.

Creative Writing

IT'S LANGUAGE ARTS THAT'S the best part of middle school for me.

My nose is always in a book outside of school anyway—sometimes literally, because *how could you not smell that wonderful new-book smell?*—and so reading and studying reading and writing about reading is heaven for me. We talk about Shakespeare and Roald Dahl, we read play scripts, and some of us get picked for special book reports that involve making our own books with construction paper.

I am in ultra-heaven when we begin our lesson on creative writing.

My hands are shaking as a treasure chest of information spills out from our schoolbook. Elements of storytelling, plot outlining, and character traits are in little boxes and bullet-point lists like pieces of gold. So wonderfully neat and organized. Later I'm going to ask my mom if it's possible in any way to find and purchase this book, because it is like a bible to me. I, who will beg anyone who isn't busy to take me to Borders bookstore, whose Christmas and birthday lists consist of next installments in the *Warriors* or *The Amazing Days of Abby Hayes* series, who

wrote a tiny book of stapled-together notebook paper in kindergarten to read aloud to the class, now hold in my hands the
secret to it all.

We are then assigned some minutes of silent reading to go over
a creative nonfiction writing sample at the end of chapter 4. My
heart jumps: I see the words "Splash Mountain."

And when I read it—there's really no other way to put it—I
am changed.

I am no longer in a room of shuffling pages and the too-loud
tick tick tick of the clock. This sample, put together by who I am
thinking must be a master, instills in me feelings that make me the
most alive I've felt in a while. Probably the most alive I've felt since
starting sixth grade. This reads like one of my adventure books,
and yet it's about something I love, something I'm familiar with. I
never knew that a simple description of riding a ride could be so
… *this*. That tension could be drawn out so well, that little details in
ride animatronics or the cold shock of water could be so vivid I can
imagine myself there. And the description of the impending final
hill at the end of the ride makes me breathe faster in anticipation.
I am inside the story, sucked out of my metal chair and into the
book between the letters.

It's too soon when we are pulled back to reality to discuss it.
I don't know how to articulate the rainbow neon swirl of feeling
happening inside me, and so I sit, reeling in the best way.

But I am fixated without any hope of going back. I spend
weeks rereading this page-long piece, reliving the feelings and
returning to Disneyland via black letters on a white page. It is a
magic created with words.

After returning to it so many times, I begin to identify a flicker
in the back of my brain. It makes me want to jump onto a table, or
run down the middle of an empty street, or go to everyone I've
ever had trouble articulating feelings to and shove this book in
front of them saying, *This is why I love Disneyland so much. This is
how I feel!*

I want to make word magic too.

Another Dimension

HER EYES ARE EAGER and intense, the spooky beige-pink tower with its crumbling design providing an appropriate backdrop to her expression. It is one of those teenager rides, the Tower of Terror, the kind that big sisters and brothers go on. I think about the promotional clip from our Disneyland VHS, five terrified people standing in a narrow elevator as it drops out of sight, Mickey hat fluttering and lost in the shaft above.

"I don't want to go alone," my sister is telling me. "Zaj, you don't actually stand in the ride. You sit down during the drop. Drops, actually—it's more than one, but not a lot."

This does not make me feel better.

I dither and whine, and we go back and forth like this several times. As we do, we are ever so slightly moving through the masses of California Adventure closer to the spooky weird beige-pink tower. Scents of candy and sunscreen intermix with the brush of fabric and the occasional stroller or balloon and my sister's hand grips my wrist, the only constant. The screams of the riders are more piercing every time the giant doors at the top open and expose them to the outside. This is not a ride for me, even if I am tall enough.

Before I am ready it is looming in front of us. Now I have to make a choice. My stomach has turned to liquid and my hands are shaking. The wait time says thirteen minutes. "Not bad at all," our mom comments.

I turn to give her a look. I thought she was on my side. She only shrugs with a smile.

I freeze right before the entrance to the queue, where Disney cast members stand dressed as bellhops and people file into what looks like a decrepit hotel lobby. I bite my lip and gaze up at the tower.

My sister's hand closes around mine. "You'll be safe, I promise."

MAYBE IT'S THE AMBIENCE, starting in the queue outside as you wind between tall pillars and an overgrowth of plants. Maybe it's the story behind the Hollywood Tower Hotel created for the ride and emulated in a hotel lobby made to look frozen in 1939. Or perhaps it's the waves of distant 1930s jazz floating overhead through hidden speakers. It could be the element of the unknown, that hint of mystery, after you watch the Twilight Zone clip in the replica of a dusty library and move through what is designed to look like a dim boiler room underneath the lobby, or the build of tension while you wait for the elevator doors to welcome you into empty metal seats with only a lap belt to hold you down. Maybe it's the build of suspense and the sense of immersion into the episode itself, how easy it is to believe Rod Serling's narration when he says, *You're traveling into another dimension,* while your stomach disappears with each drop.

It could be a combination of these things. But something about it makes one ride become two, and two become more and more, and soon I'm understanding what my sister said. And—if I had to admit it—that she was right. The step into this unknown makes my body shake each time, but I cannot get enough.

I am safe. I knew I would be. And whenever we're somewhere in the park and it's quiet, the 1930s jazz floats back into my ears and I want to ask her to ride it with me again.

Weather & Cloud Types
Science Homework—2/6/06

Cirrus: A high-level cloud composed of ice crystals typically found higher than twenty thousand feet. Sometimes referred to as *mare's tails*, these look like seagull feathers found by the Pacific Ocean, or a mother's hair if it were not henna-dyed red but white.

Altostratus: Like a soft blanket, this midlevel cloud rests in mainly a blue-gray layer over the sky, sometimes producing rain. What you see on Gresham's gray days, some lighter than others.

Cumulus: Flat on the bottom, which usually start at around a thousand feet, and puffy on top. The kind people, or teachers who say they're "not an artist," mostly draw in class. Sometimes they'll build in an upward movement, like a growing stack of meteorology books on a small desk. They look friendly on sunny days—similar to the ones in the Albuquerque desert—but look at their towering height and dark base too long and soon they will resemble cumulonimbus.

Stratus: These will rest over your head in a moody way, and if low enough the fog will make you feel like you are in a scene from *Sleepy Hollow*.

Nimbus: Laden and dense with moisture and precipitation. If you visit Florida in the summer, they come every day at exactly the same time, ready to threaten lightning.

Cumulonimbus: The clouds that tornadoes are born in. These will gather and turn green in bad-weather nightmares that come from reading too many weather and natural disaster books. These will give you a paralyzing fear of one-in-a-million chance lightning strikes. But they're also the ones to stand underneath at a water park in Florida, gliding down a waterslide during a bang of thunder as you try to defy your fear.

Tornado Dreams

OUR 1970s DREAM DICTIONARY more or less describes "cyclone" dreams as "warnings against taking risks of any kind for a minimum of six months." With how terrified these dreams make me feel, and how often they keep creeping up in my nightmares, I thought I'd have found a stronger meaning. Or at least one more relevant to someone who generally doesn't take risks. Standing here at our bookshelf lined with fantasy novels, history books and crystal guides leaning against one another behind scattered dried flower petals, I'm almost underwhelmed. The dark, dense cumulonimbus nightmares with impossibly fast winds and faraway storm shelters won't stop, and I'm thinking: *Risks of what? Of attempting a level-seven skill on vault I'm not ready for, like a Yurchenko, or going for a back walkover on beam without asking for a spot? Of singing louder in choir and showing how good I actually am? Of going to sit at the boys' table at lunch like I tried once in elementary school, even though boys are freakishly different at eleven? Of holding eye contact and talking more with my dad's church friends when he introduces us?* I don't take risks. I reside in a cushioned headspace of caution, planning, and overpreparation.

I conclude that I am just wasting too much time with my *Disasters* book. Its cover is cracked and frayed—"Like it's actually been in a disaster," my sister jokes—from reading and rereading. Krakatoa and Vesuvius, tsunamis and the Titanic, the 1906 San Francisco earthquake, and, of course, how to prepare for an emergency; it's all too intriguing to put down. I'm spending too much time learning about things that happened before in other places and preparing for what doesn't happen here in Oregon, when I ought to be doing my fractions homework and that research project for science. The stories of history that I can't stop reading are weaving their way into my dreams and trans-forming into worry and preoccupation. A useless kind. I do believe that some dreams are symbolic, sure—but I, the eleven-year-old realist/analyst, know that many are merely subconscious. I'm not a risk-taker anyway. If anything, my obsession with unrelated study itself is too much of a risk. So. Away with the book.

THE BAD DREAMS KEEP happening, even after I stop reading the *Disasters* book despite its pull and the itch in my fingers. They're the kinds of nightmares where you think you're awake, and you find yourself watching in horror as the clouds turn that telltale sickly green color and start rotating in a monstrously slow swirl that confirm your greatest fear of *a tornado in Oregon, happening for* real *this time, just like in my dreams.* I feel the nausea of terror and alarm and I start running to the nearest shelter I can find with a cellar, basement, anything to hide in or under—*But where's my family?*—and right as the winds pick up and I see it touch down in the distance is when I wake in reality. This is usually when I think again about how much of a risk-taker I am not.

Skill

FOUR INCHES TO LAND it: two hands, two feet, in a rhythm exacted, one after the other and timed just right. Squared hips, arms high, and it will be landed.

A cartwheel—simple, really, the mechanics of a circle over a beam. Physics will tell you that it can be done in one smooth flow.

Yet a single muscle's errant nudge, a single shoulder tilted out of line, a single anxious *What if I …* when inverted, and the wheel wobbles on its axis, taking the roll with it and falling out of line four feet to the ground to a defeated, but still safe, landing.

What Is Homeschooling?

IT HAS BEEN MONTHS, and it's still a strange shift. Maybe if I write it down, it'll make more sense:

> Homeschooling means an alternative form of education that takes place in the home, with parents or tutors as instructors, instead of traditional public or private schooling. It means that feeling of importance and freedom on the day you get your official homeschooling card in the mail, with the correct spelling of your name on it, recognized by the school district.

> It means shifting back into the person you were before middle school began, away from the person you felt yourself turning into. Away from someone who was a combination of everyone else, who cared about lip gloss and brand names, who laughed off insults that cut too deep and was rude to friends because it was cool. Away from shoving and punching for fun and taking notes in a format that made no sense. It means no more metal lockers, no more invitations to Talented and Gifted events during class and having to explain to your uninvited friends, who by those rules were apparently neither talented nor gifted,

that the invitations meant nothing and the yellow paper was not special. No more being pulled aside for advanced reading and writing assignments.

It also means choosing what you want to learn about and having all the time you desire for your fixations. Natural disasters and biology, Aztec and Mayan civilizations, the rules of grammar and syntax; all of the mythology books you can get your hands on, all of the ancient Egypt books and brochures and real papyrus from your sister's adventure. It means only gymnastics friends and their birthday parties and sleepovers. It means wearing what you are comfortable in, loose clothes and slip-on shoes when you're not in a leotard and shorts, without having to worry about what others think.

It means assisting at the school where your mom works, wearing a constant *Ask me for help!* smile for the children, or going with your sister to her Tae Kwon Do practice, hovering above the floor in a middle split while everyone shouts with their hits and kicks. It means having three teachers called Mom, Dad, and Big Sister and reading used college textbooks on anatomy and astronomy. It means going to Disneyland three times in one year when, somehow, things go right with money.

But most of all, it means more time. More time to make your own schedule and to learn without worrying about other people; more time to organize notes the way you need and read the books you want to read. More time to finally write those stories.

Jerry has appeared on my lap in the middle of my writing. I pet him, taking a break. Maybe it makes a little more sense now? I am not sure, but I do like what I have to look forward to.

Things I Only Do as a Preteen

I only wear baseball caps if they have SpongeBob or the *Pirates of the Caribbean* logo on them.

I only keep my hair in braids, because any other way is too complicated to deal with.

I only wear shoes with a heel for the most special of occasions, because I hate heels for the way they make my back feel and the way they are not me.

I only read teen books if they have no romance, because too often it makes characters act irrationally.

I only put on makeup if I'm dressing up for fun.

I only listen to movie soundtracks, and *maybe* radio songs if I can't predict where they're going to go.

I only sing when I'm alone or with the cats (and that one time my dad thought I was, standing next to him at his church, I was just moving my mouth).

I only talk to new people if a smile isn't enough and I have a prepared script in my head.

Or to answer the little kid asking me if I am a girl or a boy.

I only work on my book project after schooling sessions, as a reward for studying so hard.

And I only write stories that end on happy notes.

Composition

But have you really listened to those songs?

You are taken to another universe, another land, within the interlocking notes of Hans Zimmer and James Newton Howard's film scores, pulled away from your creaking wooden desk under the sparkly purple lamp until all that exists as far as you know are the universes of *Batman Begins* and *The Dark Knight* and *The Prestige* and *Pirates of the Caribbean,* as well as the one you're creating on the page with your cramped left hand; and it is not just the exciting crash of cymbals and brass that sweeps you into ships and sailing or dark city streets and shadowed alleyways—no, it's that subtler stuff that *really* gets you, the stuff composed so precisely to convey emotion, the stuff that reaches into hidden parts inside that you can only get to via music or nature, hidden parts that you only discover exist when there's this flare of bluish-gold synesthetic feeling radiating from just below your heart that comes out in goose bumps; it's the composition and combination of notes that not only reminds you of exactly where they come in the movie, but also for some reason make you envision an open and unclaimed field with tall grasses or a forest clearing, silently sunlit and golden, and it's *this* feeling right here that drives the pencil so fast that your left hand is cramped and you have no choice but to switch hands to write—though it's okay because you've been practicing—because the words and universe are coming out too fast from the music.

The Intricacies of Social Interaction

MY SISTER HAS HAD so many friends, too many to count. And they are always nice. When we lived in Albuquerque, I remember laughing as one of them tossed me above his head, giving me that tickly weightless sensation in my stomach. Once we moved to Gresham she amassed a collection quickly, from school and Tae Kwon Do and dance and everything else she's involved in that I have a hard time keeping track of. I even cried once because one was over at our house once and wanted to give me a hug before he left, but I was upstairs. It was *so kind* of him, because I'd only just met him that day, and how can people be so kind?

My sister's room is like mine in that it's got all sorts of things stuck to the walls with tape and thumbtacks, posters and magazine pictures and art; where she has *The Matrix* and *Romeo + Juliet*, I have *Charlie and the Chocolate Factory* and *Corpse Bride*. Where she has boy band pictures and Renaissance art, I've got Nickelodeon Magazine covers and wobbly-lined family scenes I drew in kindergarten. Where she has Polaroid photos from parties taped to her red-and-gold walls, I have third- through fifth-grade class pictures with hearts around my friends' faces as well as photos from my Albuquerque preschool classes. My face in one preschool photo, lowered and showing teeth but not quite smiling, is colored blue in angry jagged marker lines. Nowadays I shake my head when I look at it, recalling the spurt of anger I felt at my four-year-old inability to smile on command like everyone else.

I like to look at my sister's photos whenever I'm in her room, either sitting on her shiny smooth comforter or leaning in her doorway when we talk. The photos of her and her friends are both in day- and nighttime, and everyone's grinning with either their whole face or just their eyes. I like to look closely at the way they hold their bodies, the ease with which they sit or stand or have their arms raised, and I try to emulate that ease.

I AM WITH MY sister and her friends at a Thai restaurant after her Tae Kwon Do practice, and between bites I'm observing and taking mental notes like usual: the lilt of their voices in casual speak, the rise of an eyebrow when making a joke, the blank look during a moment of sarcasm, how they sit, how they stand, how they gesture. I study people so often that I don't notice it, and I'm so involved in my surreptitious observations that I'm caught off guard when one of her friends turns to me.

"So, Zaj." She takes a bite of noodles. "How's gym been going?"

I reach into my mental inventory, to all of the information I've gathered thus far about answering questions. This is it—a chance to be like them, like everyone else. And yet there's just so much information.

I smile and feel my eyes dart around, shrugging. Reverting. "Good."

My sister's friend nods. "Feel ready for your meet?" *She's so nice.*

I look at my sister. Eyes, so many eyes on me. My gaze flicks back to the spring rolls I have in front of me. "I think so." Feeling daring, I raise my eyebrows and tilt my head and add, "I hope so."

There. A kind-of joke? I giggle and shrug, wondering why it's all so difficult.

But they laugh. An easy laugh that I can join. I feel like I've won something, though I don't know what exactly.

"No, you're definitely ready." My sister nods, and then they discuss gymnastics practice. It's a conversation I take part in somewhat well, albeit minimally.

Every time I look down at my plate, my hands—somewhere safe—I try to relax my residual tenseness. Why is it so easy to slip into what's comfortable? To act like a child even though I'm thirteen? To wait for someone else to speak for me? Why are things suddenly harder now that I am older?

Next time, I tell myself as I crunch on a spring roll. *I can plan for next time; I can be brave and confident and easy like my sister and her friends.*

And I should try that kind-of joke thing again.

How Old

I AM IN SEASIDE, on the sidewalk circling the statue declaring the end of the journey for those two explorers I study almost obsessively in my homeschooling—Lewis and Clark—with my dad. We're making our way to the steps that lead down into the sand where I can feel it fold warmly over my feet before the shock of the cold Pacific seawater. But first we have to make it through the throng of cars and people, past the moms and dads and children lathered in sunscreen carrying their beach towels and flip-flops, past the couples with their digital cameras by the railing, past the group lounging by the statue and Seaside, Oregon, sign in their multicolored swim trunks watching us, locs bobbing when they nod and say, "That's a nice girl you got there" to my dad. My dad has to then put his big protective arms around my shoulders and say, "That's my *daughter*" as we hurry away; we have to laugh, flustered and a little weirded out when we round the corner.

And then I have to think, *How old do I look?* and consider maybe my height or the clothes I'm wearing or the ocean-ready skin I'm showing before getting to the sandy concrete steps so I can be a kid again, which is funny because I don't know when I switched out of being a kid. Then, and only then, can I finally feel the warm sunbaked sand fold over my feet and between my toes, burying itself under itself like the memory of the group in the throng of the beach crowd.

I AM IN THE Lloyd Center mall and need to wait outside a RadioShack because of the Christmastime *it's a secret* barring my entrance. I need to wait for however long and try not to get bored or maybe overwhelmed in the lights-people-noise of the mall, and so I will just lean against the wall to people-watch. I'll be sure not to meet anyone's eyes, no matter how close they get. Like this tall guy with a crooked baseball cap. Because if we see each other, the next thing he'll do after sipping from his half-full McDonald's cup is talk to me—

Well, there I go. I was too nervous, and I did. That was my fault. First I'll have to laugh when he asks if I got in trouble and had to wait outside because of it. Then, because I hardly understand him the first time, I'll need to ask him to repeat himself when he asks, "So how *old* is you?" But now my face is burning and my heart is racing, so I need to mutter something and try to be uninteresting so he'll go away and stop saying things I can't understand in the din and the way he speaks. I definitely need to frown when he asks, "Is you eighteen?" because I am clearly wearing a Jonas Brothers T-shirt and am a kid (aren't I?). But then I need to consider my height, which I can't help, and perhaps the fact that I am smiling too much, which seems like an encouragement but which I can't help either because it is a nervous impulse.

I don't actually know what I need to do now. I turn pleading eyes to the strangers around us for guidance. They breeze past, some with little more than a glance. Like they don't want to touch us.

Oh, there—I'm almost done—before leaving I only have to go back to being quiet again, this time a relieved quiet. Because now, I just have to stay a little behind while my mom uses her *my daughter* words and energy to shove the guy with the McDonald's cup and baseball cap away, then watch his back as he saunters and tugs at his sagging pants while he tries to laugh. And I need to think about more important things, like what secrets are concealed in that RadioShack bag, rather than the phantom sense of shame, because I have no idea where it came from and it's already gone with the guy in the crowd.

If

THEY SAY IT IS a good idea for writers to keep a personal journal. I already have journals for dreams, plot outlines, character traits, random ideas, and then a stack of blank unused ones. But having read that it's ideal to keep a diary of thoughts and feelings, I pick up a small yellow composition notebook.

I wish there were more hours in the day. If I became a hermit, I would get more of my book done.

Though I do like people. If I listened to pop music and wore clothes that hugged my skin and acted the way girls my age act, I could make more friends. Like the girls in optionals, all huddled in clouds of chalk by the bars or off to the side of the vault runway giggling over inside jokes. I feel like they speak a secret language that I don't understand.

If I weren't so tall for my age older boys and men would probably leave me alone. I wouldn't walk so awkwardly, and my sister-coach wouldn't be having a harder time spotting me in the skills that are keeping me from moving out of level six to optionals.

If I didn't care so much about numbers, I wouldn't soak them into my being and feel myself a walking 9.25/10 or an awful 7.5/10. I wouldn't think about money and the cost of things; I wouldn't still feel the weight of an ugly bronze medal of a 3.2 GPA I was awarded in sixth grade, when my classmates got silver and gold for higher grades.

If I weren't so scared about my back mobility issues and knew how to handle my height during dynamic movements like tumbling, I would finally move up to level seven. I could choose my own floor music instead of dancing to the same level-six song that plays in my sleep. If I could just find a way to perform the dance without the anxiety of scores and numbers, of competition, of *this is it, don't mess up, don't self-sabotage, don't let anyone down,* especially *not your sister-coach.*

If I could be as outgoing as my sister, as confident and outspoken as her, I could make the feelings I have into something like sentences. I would be a better volunteer at the school my mom works at and not get embarrassed when little kids ask me questions I don't know the answer to.

I could say the things I need to say, but can't. Not yet.

CLOSING THE YELLOW COMPOSITION notebook, I reach across my desk and grab the purple plot outline one. Mentally, it's much more stimulating.

Conversations

THE SKY TALKS TO me.

Its clouds tell me about impermanence as I watch patches of them overhead through my bedroom window, wisps of nimbostratus cotton pulling apart to make a momentary break in the gray and white and reveal the light blueness of spring. The sky makes me a promise:

It promises that things are not permanent, to fall in love with the moments that seem unchanging, because it is all part of the shifting.

The trees talk to me.

They tell me about how they bend into the strongest gusts of wind, how the sturdiest and tallest of them like the cedar on the edge of our backyard let their branches creak or sometimes break, how they let foliage fall and blow away, far and out of reach forever.

They also tell me about their eagerness to push the bright green growth from the new room they made.

The feral cat talks to me.

Ears perked and steps light, Ash/Abby is always content. Even when I glance outside and see him alone; even when we are in the yard with him but have to leave when it starts to rain. He glides with ease from one moment to the next, lifting his tranquil gaze to meet my own. We don't know when we will see each other next, and he's okay with that.

Worlds at My Fingers

IN THE BLUE BINDER on my desk rests a growing stack of pages—I think it's close to a hundred now—soft, dog-eared, and smudged with the left-hand writer's smudge; lines and lines of graphite lands with never-ending forests, gatekeeping birds, evil oceans, pirates, fantasy creatures, and steadfast friendships; words in gray building worlds in color; scribbles neat or hasty for when ideas are pouring out too fast; scratched-out sections in pencil that shine; yellow highlighter over words like *gatekeeper, panther, deep forest, Janey,* and *sailing*; sketches of trees in corners, sketches of cat eyes in margins; purple pen underlining and noting small *i*'s for typing later in italics, asterisks and arrows and footnotes ("she should be brought to the brig <u>before</u> meeting the deckhand for the first time—switch these sections"); and, most present of all, a pulling from the desk when too far away, insistent and unseen.

Cutting the Blackberry Bushes

SOMETHING IS STARTING TO weave its prickly way ever closer through my mind, in thorny tendrils like these blackberry bushes.

I stand chopping and chopping in the summer sun, my wide-brimmed hat offering only small relief to the heat. I am alone out here, in the midst of our yard being slowly overgrown and overtaken with these stupid blackberry bushes. They don't end, ever. I stop, pluck a hidden overripe berry; it is sweet and gushing.

This meet is coming up, as well as this back walkover on beam, this flyaway dismount on bars, and this roundoff back handspring back tuck. Everyone's counting on me for the uneven bars because it is my best event, counting secondly on my floor routine because of my dance skill, and placing hope in the fact that I've been tumbling well despite the brick wall of mental blocks. They can count on me.

I wipe my forehead and start chopping again. The vines are thick, often defying the sharpness of my hedge clippers and refusing to be snapped in two. It takes wriggling and pulling, yanking and tugging, before the green fibers finally tear away from each other. It's like the more I chop them back and away from our circle of backyard, the more there are. I find myself secretly wishing for the container of chemicals that our granddad sprayed with such ease on his last visit here. How, just days after, the strong thick arches of thorns turned brown and brittle. It made me shiver.

The voices of sparrows and robins provide a background to my rustling. Anxiety in the form of nausea threatens and I shove it down in a way I know well by now. But it's really just nerves. I concentrate instead on the excitement that comes with our purple team leotards, the smell of hairspray, and competition-day photos with my team. In the monotony of cutting I enter a hazy state, trying visualization like my sister taught us at practice and imagining myself throwing that back tuck, easing into that back walkover without a spot and doing everything else perfectly. It has helped me during practice several times, when I can grab hold of my brain long enough. I tell myself that I don't need anyone to spot me (a major deduction in a meet). A vine reaching straight in front of me becomes the balance beam; the flat shadowed leaves between thorns become the carpeted springboard floor.

I love this; I really do. Because I am good and getting better and competition is the point of it all and it's what everyone else loves about it, too. The *something* that I keep wanting to say about it all is just that—that I'm as excited as I should be, and I love the pressure. I'm just nervous. No other voice to be found; it doesn't exist.

One of the vines jabs into my hat from above. I hadn't noticed it before. It's protruding and creepy and startled me so much that my heart's pounding, so I attack it with the blades. I blink in all these things that don't seem to end: the heat, the nerves, the vines. Looking for that sweet hidden jewel—I know it's there—of *I love the pressure*, I chop, and I chop.

Balancing It All Out

HE IS ONE OF the few who comes inside the Gresham house. He walks on our creaking floors; he sits at our dining room table by the heater that works most of the time; he jokes with me and compliments my mom's cooking.

Sooner than I realize, one visit becomes more, and more become many. The memory of my mom's coming-home smell from the mysterious grown-up clubs has faded.

HE FIXES THE ROOF out the back door, which is near collapsing. We watch him from the kitchen as he hammers from the top of a ladder just outside, wobbling and determined.

He helps make the floor in the downstairs bathroom more solid somehow so we don't nearly sink into it every time we take a shower or bath. I didn't know it was something that could be fixed.

He chops pounds and pounds of wood, moving like a machine. His red flannel folds like my sister's.

He brings his dogs over to run in our yard, big slobbering goofy things whose tongues aren't scratchy and whose voices are loud. Their bodies are funny, clumsy masses: one black, one brown.

In the winter he builds a tiny outdoor house for Ash/Abby,

who is sick, even though he is viciously allergic to cats. The house is made out of an overturned yellow recycling container and old towels.

Each time, he backs his maroon-colored Ford Explorer out of our driveway until next time.

IN HIS HOUSE, THE first thing I notice is the lack of a fireplace. Or a heater. There's *internal heating* that you set the temperature to. Like at my dad's house. Meaning: we don't have to do all this wood chopping or *will it turn on yet?* heater whacking.

The second thing I notice is the lack of bugs in the corners. No spiders. No long-legs. No ants. Meaning: we can forget about a cereal box left open and not worry about a Huge Ant Problem in the morning.

The third thing I notice is the size of the house. It's like half the size of ours. I can't do leaps in the kitchen, and our all-but-broken trampoline would take up most of this backyard. But we don't have to huddle under piles of blankets at night to keep warm, or caulk the corners to keep bugs and wind out. Instead, we press a couple of buttons on the thermostat and make sure the sliding glass windows are shut all the way.

I STAND AT A window upstairs overlooking the busy Columbia Boulevard, an echo of cars replacing the creak of tree branches and rustle of wind through tall grasses, in the bedroom that is meant to be mine soon—too fast, we are moving too fast—and hold strong like the trunk of our tall cedar.

It's as if going through the I-84 portal to Portland has made houses both newer and smaller, along with the rest of the world.

Mirror, I Have Some Questions

Promise it stays between us, okay?

I just want to know: What will I look like when I'm older? Will this boylike long-torso gymnast body stay like this the rest of my life? Will I still be tall for my age, so tall that older boys will keep trying to talk to me? Will my walk still be awkward and stiff with too much of a forward lean and weight in my steps? Will I always stand in front of you like this, trying to make a front chunk of my hair into a side-swoop of braid-bangs that hangs perfectly over my eyebrows? Do I need to keep wearing bandanas to cover my forehead that incessantly, indignantly keeps breaking out? And will my eyebrows always be like this—so thick I need to pluck away where they meet in the middle but dark enough to contrast just right against my skin?

Speaking of skin—and you must betray this to no one—will I always look like this? Will I always have to explain to people that I am not immune to sunburns? Or have to feel guilty about worrying when I approach a person who is Black instead of half-Black and prepare either for the deep disgust, high admiration, or blatant staring when they see the way my skin is fairer than their own?

Mirror, I have to know: What will stay constant? What will struggle to change?

If I wish hard enough and stare into you for so long that my vision goes wavy, will it make you wavy too, enough that I can make things change? I see flickers of something like beauty, if I tilt my head just so or hold a light beneath my face a certain way—but how do I get there? Can you tell me how? Can you show a future me?

There is the last braid. I have to go. But I'll be back to wish and ask.

Pushing the Car Home in the Snow

SNOW, KNEE-HIGH IN SOME places, crunches under my feet in wet clumps of white and gray. But I am sweating under my coat pushing this old, old car and bothered that I have to push this old old car, but I must because it's like as old as I am and somehow still turning on enough for us to have driven it to Fred Meyer but break down on the way back. My sister from inside leans out the window and tells me to use my triceps-deltoids-abdominals and so I huff and press my palms against the faded red bumper of the Ford Tempo. The snow is bright and the monotony of the effort and silence of the street is like a tunnel slide for a wandering mind and I wonder at the sheer weight of a car, if plastic bags filled with ingredients for a pasta dinner for two can perhaps make a significant difference. As we round the corner, suddenly ever nearer finally to the house, pride comes up out of nowhere—we're doing it, just me and her making it all the way back from Fred Meyer to the house, we're going to have made it all this way—but then just as quickly it disappears as a man passes by in his truck and offers to help. Relieved, and weirdly disappointed, I hop in our car. We are quiet and focused during his steady push all the way down Palmblad Road under the towering green-and-snow-white trees, back to the house. Inside, it has never felt so warm, the classical music from our speakers so pleasant, and our homemade fancy pasta dinner so savory, especially when I think about how, really, it was mostly the two of us who got the car home.

We Will Be Safe

I HAD THIS DREAM the other night, right before waking up early
to go with my mom to the middle school she worked at.

Actually, no, not quite. It was one of those waking dreams,
where you think you've woken up but you're still caught in
between and the elements of your dream walk around you like
shadows.

I was standing atop Mount Hood with a little kid who was lost.
He wore a shirt that swirled in colors that I couldn't name, which
only existed in this dream-not-dream. I held hands with him as we
stood there kind of wobbling, and I was trying to get him to follow
me: home was this way. I was seeing the familiar mountain, which
I see on our horizon every day, from the opposite side, which I'd
only ever seen once before in my life when we passed it driving
from the west side of Oregon. Its stark blues and whites coupled
with my lack of balance terrified me. It was so *there*, too there. And
it was silent, yet the sun radiating off the peak was very loud in its
brightness.

I felt a foreign sense of protectiveness over this little boy. Like
how I feel toward Jerry. Mother-like. I squeezed his hand and he

squeezed back, tugging a little behind me. I smiled despite my terror. "We will be safe," I said.

To glance up and over Mount Hood's peak at more snow and rocks made me dizzy. I stumbled. There was a knowledge that somehow I'd be fine, that I could fly or was probably a giant or some other dream thing, but still. I had to be careful.

The sky transformed into the purple of my bedroom ceiling. Things were dissipating. We had to hurry.

So, quickly, I got ready to jump, pulling him into my arms even though he really, *really* didn't want to.

When my mom came in my room and put in my movie soundtrack CD to wake me up for real, I found that my arm muscles were tensing, still feeling the shadow-child in my arms.

So What?

IF THE GAPS IN the corners of the house are growing wider,

if the septic tank needs tending to more and more, and the downstairs bathroom is still sinking into the ground,

if the upstairs bathroom is hardly a bathroom with an unusable sink and a toilet that doesn't always flush,

if it is the kind of cold that is *cold* during winter,

if it takes some effort to maintain the slowly claiming overgrowth,

if the front door squeaks too loudly when it opens or the living room floor is so uneven that pencils and rubber balls roll to the middle?

And so what if the presence of nonhuman creatures feels a little too close or the tree branches outside the window creak too much when the wind blows hard,

if the house is becoming nature's home?

So what?

So *what* if the house is "falling apart"?

It isn't. It's ours.

The Shed

PAST THE BARRIER OF cedar trees under which our tire swing hangs and our white wire archway stands at a slant is the back part of the property with the blueberry bushes, the grapevine, the clothesline, the greenhouse, the sea of blackberry thorns, and then that shed. Its caving roof hovers over all the junk my uncles who lived here before us piled in there. It is so filled with crawling things and sharp, jagged edges that it takes me a while to join my mom and sister in one of their ventures to look inside. I see comics, VHS tapes, cassettes, baseball cards, a radio that works, a TV that doesn't, books with no covers, guitar picks. All torn, broken, waterlogged, stained and covered in dust and memories I do not know but imagine. It's falling apart, the shed, but it still stands. A presence since we moved in, refusing to give.

WE WILL SOON BE returning to that shed to clear out the rest of what we want as much before we are gone, which is something I choose not to think about. I am in my Indiana Jones obsession, and I've become an adventurer, the back half of the property an unknown land to be explored. I'm wearing my black woven fedora and my small canvas messenger bag. It contains a notebook and pencil for recording my findings, my compass, my Indiana Jones notebook from Borders with the map inside, and, of course, a water bottle. I never do well in the heat, which is funny for a New Mexican.

My steps are large over the grasses that both arc over my head and pile under my feet. If I didn't know this place like the back of my hand, I'd feel lost. Left, right, and ahead is grass both lush and thin, thick and faded, green and brittle yellow. Infinite like a cornfield maze. There is no noise but for me and the *shhh* of the breeze through the stalks. Overactive fancies in my brain spark and rise, combining into plotlines and stories to accompany my walk through the pulsating silence of the yard.

I imagine.

The shed is a temple, similar to the one in the second Indiana Jones film or the ride at Disneyland. Goose bumps rise in a sudden, steady wave on my arms and my breath catches. Maybe I will find relics inside from a past I don't understand. A past that can reveal more about the future. Because isn't that one of the reasons we study history — to tell us about the possibilities of the future? Or so that we don't repeat history's mistakes? Something like that. I stop to check the map, take a sip of water, and keep going. A glance behind reveals nothing but grasses taller than my head. With every step I take toward the temple hidden somewhere in this strange land, my home and current life rest behind me and shrink in size. If I keep walking forward, will the house disappear entirely? Will my current life go with it and vanish from existence?

I wish Ash/Abby were here. I don't know where he's been lately. This is his home. I always imagined him as my companion on these ventures, trotting beside me and weaving effortlessly between the grasses. But maybe a tiger, or a panther, will emerge instead. Maybe there's a whole city of cats like a dream I had once. But there—I think I see it. The temple.

I step and push the grasses aside at a faster pace. It's even more dilapidated than I was expecting. The house and the real world behind me are so small they are nearly forgotten. The shed looks like it's waiting for me, still there and standing, a brown slant between the wavering stalks.

Brightly Muted

I'M STARTING TO LIKE new things. That one Green Day song about walking alone. The screech and drone of electric guitar like the one my uncle plays. Tim Burton movies. *Sweeney Todd.* Minor keys. I can't stand pop music or the color pink, and I am exasperated when romance comes up in the teen books I read because I can't relate. I jump into the pool of films and music I enjoy—the only pool I'm not afraid to get my head under—and swim, further and further away from what I am supposed to like as an early-teen girl. I find comfort in this pool of new things, escape in it when things around me move and change too fast.

But I also love the softness of Jerry's fur when he settles in my lap in front of the downstairs heater. I love blowing dandelions and making secret wishes that have to do with time travel and bravery. I love plucking the tiny buttercups in our yard to make bouquets, admiring how they are yellow like our favorite flavored popcorn. I love writing stories about little squirrels and cheerful cats and will read any story with a happy ending. And I am becoming more and more enchanted by the stage and especially by *The Nutcracker* ballet. These are constant and unchanging: they have to be.

People search for a box, or a category, into which I can be

placed. They attempt to pin me down and understand. I do, too. But I can't find a label. These opposites are swirling around in me, pushing, forming, pulling, molding. Opposites like heavy and light, black and white, all at once and also a lot of other things. And so I keep sitting outside in the sun listening to songs with the shadows of minor keys.

With every replay of that Green Day song, with every night-time gaze out the car window to find comfort in the dark empty lots, with every clothing choice of muted color over bright, words hover in the background. They wait, urgent and quivering behind my teeth, for me to understand them.

Value

Vault: 8.5
Floor: 9.0

My value was once aligned with numbers earned—equal and solid, boxed in, black digits over white: a mirror for the self, self-image ranked by a finite scale.

Beam: 8.5
Bars: 9.25
All-around: 35.25

My value, I see now, lies in an ever-expanding, ever-changing topography that is determined by no number, determined by no score, determined by no one but myself.

Athlete's Pride

THE WALL IN MY mind is in pieces.

It's not quite the one I thought it was, a barrier for words I wanted to say about myself and my growing interest in new things. No, this wall was off to the side, hardly noticeable yet no less difficult to move past. It had actually been in the corner of my vision this whole time, but only now after breaking it have I noticed its presence.

I am dancing in my bedroom. It's to an instrumental song from the score of one of my favorite films, full of sweeping violin and glockenspiel and three-four counts. Dreamy Danny Elfman magic.

I am creating.

Last week, I voiced a truth that apparently was not a surprise to anyone but still needed to be said by me. The idea of letting down my team, my gym, and—most of all—my sister-coach pressed its heavy gray weight over my head. I don't know how I was able to say it—or, rather, force it out. Maybe it was the fact that it was easier because of how obviously the pressure was getting to me.

Or maybe it was the response from my sister and my mom. And after I said the fateful *I think I'm done with competing*, the shock and surprise I had braced myself for never came; it was met instead with understanding and patience. Knowing nods and calm tones.

Where the music builds for the first time here, I bring my feet together on my purple carpet and spin. But not like that—I scroll back a few seconds on my iPod to try it again.

After I said those words and realized nobody was freaking out, the relief came in light blue waves mixing with warm amber gratitude.

Though it was not without the navy-colored melancholy. I was saying goodbye to seven years of medals, seven years of high all-around and uneven bar scores, seven years of feeling the mastery of body weight inverted over four inches of beam or flipping over a vault table or leaping across blue springboard carpet.

Seven years of an athlete's pride.

I spin again. Almost. Though I guess I have more than seven years to work on things like this. More than seven years to create and recreate. To move how I want, without the pressure of numbers, scores, and getting older and taller.

There. My sister-coach always says—said—during practice that visualizing a movement before doing it would help. And, I guess, it always did; I spin smoothly, reflecting the upward glide of the strings. Yes. Now I can go on with the rest of the song.

And it comes to me: I realize that my athlete's pride is not lost with stopping gymnastics. The gymnast is still there and a part of my identity. Gymnastics has formed me into a person with all these hidden strengths that I'm still discovering. My gymnast self will be a part of me forever. And who knows—maybe I can throw in a back walkover somewhere in a dance I choreograph.

This new swoop of the cello here makes me want to do something like a swoop, too. Something big. There is a certain kind of power in making up a dance, translating music to motion and making a kind of art that's only yours. I circle my right leg through the air and take a big step, like over a heaping mound.

Straightened

No more braids. I like it. Though I can't get it wet, or else the wash/blow-dry/straightening process would be undone, an expensive hour-plus-long process gone in seconds.

But I can run my fingers through it. Smoothly. Like I've always wanted to do with the braids I tried to get so small. It grazes my shoulders, shiny with product like a teen star in a movie or a music video. I look like dark-haired celebrities. It is sleek and, when I am fresh out of the salon that specializes in Black hair or in-between hair like mine, it hugs my head and falls in a dark curtain behind my ears. Much easier to put into a ponytail or back in a headwrap at night or just comb through and let *be*. Sure, I do sometimes kind of miss my braids and how I could let those get rained on or splashed by shower droplets and just be too. But this, *this* is my new normal. My new me. My hair is straight, and I feel beautiful.

And, you know, even between hair appointments when it's in its poofed-out natural state isn't so bad, I guess. It's long enough now (!!) to keep back in a simple ponytail. Although I much prefer it silky smooth and what I feel like is perfect, there is a sense of something like freedom when I can stand in a Portland drizzle and feel okay, a sense of calm as I feel the fingers of the damp breeze threading through each individual, natural strand.

Big Adventure

MY FIRST PRACTICE AS a level seven is one of my last days as a gymnast. Technically it isn't "practice," since I'm no longer practicing for anything, but I still come to work out. As an optional, at last. It is strange to have this part of my life that defined me for years to be over. Only my closest friends, my sister-coach, and the gym owners know so far.

The beginning of practice is the same, and also completely different.

I warm up as a level seven.

I jog laps around the floor as a level seven.

I do my conditioning, sit-ups, push-ups, and leg kicks as a level seven.

Then: I choose what level-seven skills on bars and vault I would compete. I work on level-seven beam and floor choreography.

I decided on "The Breakfast Machine" from *Pee-wee's Big Adventure* for floor—the main theme, so people who knew the film and enjoyed it like me would recognize it. My sister and I had already begun working on it together at home; now I'm really able to let my body expand onto the space of the floor instead of condensing to fit a living room. Of course, there were countless other songs I had to choose over—one, apparently too "scary" according to one of the level eights, being from *The Dark Knight*— but in the end this one was perfect for a floor routine, able to be cut at a minute and a half. Plus, it's fun.

A flare of something like excitement goes up in me when the music blasts through the speakers. I'm just running through choreography—not tumbling or doing all of the skills full out yet. Like the optionals when they're working on new routines. Now I'm one of them.

As the cymbals crash, I feel the other optionals watching and I suddenly feel a flush of embarrassment. Is this song too silly? It's too silly. No sophisticated Spanish guitar or fancy swinging big-band themes. Mine's too erratic, too childish. My motions shrink.

I glance over at my sister in her coach stance with crossed arms and my friends who are new level sevens like me. I reach for the surge that ran through me the first time I moved to this song. It appears suddenly and the outside world fades; I burst through a split midair and my arms reach through each extension all the way through my fingers. Goose bumps rise as I alternate between quick and slow movements, engaging my fast-twitch muscles.

There's so much space on the floor to dance this piece.

What's Still There

ITEMS COME TO MIND immediately, though for my list I can't really differentiate which I want to keep or leave behind at the house:

Coathangers in my closet, some with too-small T-shirts I don't wear so much anymore.

My piles of stuffed toys on the shelf in my closet.

The black papasan chair in front of the downstairs heater.

That printout on my door with different WordArt versions of my name typed on it.

Old jackets hanging by the front door, including the rainbow-striped one I've had since first grade.

Fourth- and fifth-place medals from gymnastics meets.

A train, on the tracks just on the other side of Columbia Boulevard and therefore much too close to this house, blows its horn. Something shifts in my brain after I unplug my ears and let my heart rate lower.

The trampoline in the unmown backyard.

Wood chips and ashes in the fireplace.

The two very tall and thin trees at the end of the driveway that sway in strong winds.

Zaji Mountain, which stands a little forward from the foot of the trees.

The tire swing.

The feral dogs.

Ash/Abby.

Jerry and Neo. Though my dad checks on them from time to time. Plus, cats are independent.

They have each other.

The train fades. I hear the heater come on, a soft *shhh* through the vent above my head. I look up from where I sit at my desk, thinking about both heaters that no longer work at the Gresham house. About the sinking bathroom floor that cannot be fixed. About the upstairs toilet that no longer flushes. About the septic tank, about the collapsing roof, about all the things we'd been working on fixing for so long but can't be fixed, eventually making it a place too hard to live in.

I Am an Island

WE'RE PASSING BY DE La Salle North Catholic High School on our way back home from New Seasons Market. Driving by a high school reminds me of driving by Dexter McCarty all those summers ago, back when I tried to look inside the windows and see if there were lockers. Sometimes I peer between the arms of the high school's chain-link fence to the throng of students forming into tight knots or dispersing like streams, wondering what it's all like. To be around people your age, to have friends and phone numbers and papers and study groups. I send text messages to a few people from gymnastics every now and then, with a rush of excitement whenever I hear my phone buzz: *I have friends!*

I was studying for my GED, but scores and numbers are so arbitrary in terms of gauging intelligence, and I don't do well with tests anyway. So we are also talking about an actual school. But likely not a regular high school. There is a small part of me deep inside that crouches down and tries to hide whenever I think about going to regular high school. I recall sixth grade, how I didn't quite realize at the time how it was changing me into some other person entirely—someone I wasn't sure *I* would've liked. The image of eleven-year-old me trying to transform and find herself brings a gentle smile to my face.

There are many schools close to where we live now. De La Salle is very close. It is not quite a regular high school. I have a friend from gymnastics who goes there. And it's mostly made up of kids who live in neighborhoods close to ours in Kenton. They talk super loud and blast hip-hop from their phones and fire banter between each other that I can't really understand and sometimes makes me think they're arguing until I hear laughter. I see the way others who walk their dogs or stand close by their children at playgrounds look at them, shouting and laughing and being their whole selves. Obviously there's nothing wrong with them, and they always seem like a close-knit community, but ...

That's a thought I can never seem to finish. That *but* ... makes me feel bad. Slightly ashamed. I can't place the reason.

Even though I'd fit in based on appearance alone, that's about where it ends. If I went to that school, I'd feel like an island in their sea, with a weird, unexplored terrain and a culture all of my own, immersed in a culture I feel I should know well but haven't got a clue how to navigate.

But De La Salle is just one school on the list, and our search for something alternative continues. Preferably, it will be somewhere I can find people who also listen to punk rock.

Bike Path

GRAVEL POPS AND CRUNCHES under my bike tires as I slow to a stop, panting. I lift my head. Cirrus clouds slide above my head on a deep blue sky; I allow a few moments of stillness to watch them pull apart at an infinitely slow pace, morphing into new shapes in colossal humid fibers. I shudder, feeling miniscule.

The mostly gravel path snakes in front of me, slipping down into a river on the right and a golf course on the left. My thighs are burning, unused to pedaling so hard for so long on something unpaved. The biking my sister and I did in Gresham was either down the smooth Springwater Trail or through the neighborhood. The trail wound through a canopy of all kinds of trees and bushes, and if we felt adventurous we'd ride all the way to Main City Park, a long ride that felt like *miles*. Of course, my brain came up with all sorts of stories hidden if you looked close enough between the wet leaves and crow's feathers and trickling streams. In the neighborhood we'd cross Palmblad Road and pause at the corner house—the one that projected *The Nightmare Before Christmas* every Halloween on their garage door—to choose right, left, or forward. Right brought us past the newer houses, left led us to make a U through one of the many cul-de-sacs, and forward brought us down the road populated with kids. I loved that road because it felt like summer all the time, a free-for-all just for young people to skateboard and rollerblade and shoot hoops, no parents allowed. Like they lived in a cartoon world. Both the trail and the neighborhood felt intertwined yet distinct. Places we knew so well they may have been etched on our hearts. Or at least driven into our calves and quadriceps.

Here, in Portland, there are so many bike trails and paths. Mapped and marked and made for people who ride for sport and exercise. It's almost overwhelming.

"On your left." I jump as a serious cyclist breezes past me, sleek and quick on their thin serious-cyclist road bike. In a few moments they are gone. I get my feet on the pedals. I've rested enough—I'm a former gymnast, an athlete. Time to get going.

Ballet Class

POWDER—LIKE BABY POWDER—is the first thing you notice about the studio when you walk in: let it set the mood of delicacy as you ascend the carpeted stairs. Listen for the faint trickling of piano in precise three-four counts—fast or slow but almost always a waltz rhythm—as you go to sit on the old cushioned chairs or couch in the waiting area, with mothers and grandmothers and maybe a dad or two.

The teacher is a woman who wears her gray hair in a messy pile atop her head, controlling the music with a black remote from her metal foldout chair to watch every minute detail of your movement. This class is often just a handful of people, or maybe two of you or even just you. Do your best to move your body to the music in ways that feel unusual, uncomfortable, or different while you dance the choreography—sorry, combinations—that prove to be a memory test. Such long sequences. When it's you and others at the barre, in the small studio space you can peek around or in the mirror for what to do if you forget the combinations. But when it's just you there it can be a struggle, especially when you move from barre to center. Just remember how your arms go up into either fifth or first position when you soutenu turn, the leg must be rotated outward when in arabesque, you must plié and bend your knees when jumping out to second position (don't land on straight legs, duh), and keep your shoulders *down*.

Try your hardest to adopt the qualities of *light* and *airy* and *graceful*, even through the bulk of muscles that get in the way. Try, even though your stiff gymnast fingers don't flutter and float like you've seen in *The Nutcracker*. Try, even though the way you carry your upper body isn't the way ballerinas do, your motions across the creaking wood floor don't glide how you envision them in your mind, and the *combinations*, the combinations are so long and complex that you have too much to think about.

But you know what? You came prepared.

You have muscles. You can extend your leg so high it's next to your ear. You know how to engage your core and protect your body from impact; you know how to initiate movement the safe way. Your turnout is excellent and you do it right—from the hip and not the knee. And you're a rather fast learner, as it happens.

Wildflower Bouquet

THEY ARE SEATED ON the trampoline as we half-play Truth or Dare in the dusk. One weaves a flower crown out of dandelions, and the one next to him braids her hair. The rusted springs extend and contract gently under the weight of ten or so.

I was hesitant to host a party here, but the size of our group and the fact that this Gresham home is still *ours* even though we have officially moved to Portland has made this so. I am plucking dandelions and buttercups near where they sit, working on a bouquet as colorful as I can make it. I've never liked those dyed store-bought rainbow bouquets. Too artificial. I said as much to them earlier with my nose wrinkled in distaste, and they laughed. I laughed, too, a real one that wasn't forced.

Sixth grade was weird. High school is weird. However, the weird of Trillium Charter School fits me like a glove. I can wear purple-striped socks or a skinny red tie like the musicians I like and not be mocked, or I can debate with my friends for Spirit Week if boyish or extra girly is right for me for gender-swap day without being laughed at. I can choose to sit at a desk to take notes—in whatever format makes sense to my brain—or lie on the couch if there's one in the room. I can listen to my ukulele-playing teacher walking down the hall as I work on an assignment for my animal behavior class, and I can get health credit for our Tai Chi and meditation class. If it takes me longer to catch the undercurrents of nonverbal communication, or if I don't express emotion in ways people say are normal, no one cares or treats me differently. An unspoken *whatever, that's cool.*

I like lists, and so I made one of our core group when inviting them to the Gresham house party. There is:

The very tall one who wears a fedora every single day.

The one who is extremely good at sports.

The booklover who appreciates Tim Burton films and good grammar as much as I do.

The one with the patched army-green jacket.

The one I don't see much in classes and wears a lot of black.

Of course, the one I won't stop bothering about music because he also likes Muse and Tool.

The one who likes to climb on things and surprise everyone.

The one who is not embarrassed to sing and wears worn Doc Martens.

In fact, she, the jacket-wearer, and the one in black all wear worn Doc Martens.

The ones who own their uniqueness without apology and wear what they want. Which is pretty much everyone here, but still.

And then my first boyfriend. He accepts my sometimes-inexpressive face and my stiffness in carriage. He accepts my *self*. And does not talk to me like a child. He is very good with computers.

Teenage restlessness takes over. We slowly start to roam away from the trampoline. Some go to the tire swing; others go inside for cold pizza or toward the shadowed areas of the yard in close pairs or trios to explore. Memories unbidden weave around the figures of my friends. I catch a glimpse of my child self running by the hedges lining the house. She vanishes.

"Zaji." The one in black comes up to me. My heart skips a beat: she is holding Ash/Abby. "I love your cat."

IT IS NEARLY DARK and time for our group dare, a walk down the middle of the street to the Springwater Trail where my sister and I rode on our bikes so many times before. My mom and to-be stepdad tell us to be careful and watch out for "creepy creepers," but we don't have time for creeps.

The gravel driveway crunches under our feet and we spill onto the empty pavement of Palmblad Road. My boyfriend reaches for my hand, knowing how I am with initiating physical contact (I don't really), and I gladly take it. We become a huddled group of hushed chatter and loud whispers, bathed in streetlight yellow.

The one who likes to sing plucks a light pink flower from a blackberry bush and hands it to me. I didn't realize I am still holding my wildflower bouquet. "For your collection," she says.

It's the only pink one in the small bunch of color, and it is just right. I love the way mismatched things will fit perfectly together to make something imperfect.

I Still Hear the Feral Dogs

AFTER THE TRAIN COMES clunking and clanging past our house at night, I still think I can hear their voices rise again when it disappears.

When I pause between strumming Misfits chords on my guitar, I think I can hear them out my window, yipping and howling as I self-teach.

Standing on the back porch and scratching one of our dogs behind her ears, I feel the miniscule muscles twitch and imagine she's heard a distant feral bark.

After sunset on my sixteenth birthday, I think I can hear them from the playground while I lie in the curves of the corkscrew slide with my friends.

They are still a collection of ruffled, wild pelts in my mind. Still creatures of dusk and night. Yet although they are more unreachable and distant than before, I somehow feel closer to them, as if they are more present. As if I could see them if I pause and look closely between the cedar trees.

Return

IT'S A WHITE DAY as they drive down Palmblad Road, a light overcast sky hovering over the stepdad's red Volvo with the four of them inside. Everything is the same so far, after the years: the one-story yellow house on the corner, the really big almost-castle with the hedge-lined walkway to the front door, the green fence by the path leading to the school, and the constant towers of green on the sides of the road. Some newer houses intermix with the older ones, but many are the same. There is the one with the roof-climbing neighbor, and there's the one with the army-green truck and its not-broken windows. Old homes still there and going nowhere.

The portal of I-84 is really like a portal of time: the mother and daughters and stepdad have traveled from a city in flux, a city of rapid new-car motion through road construction as irregular as a stream of fashion trends, of new buildings and people and places and feelings. The ever-present *what next, create, move forward, stay current* has now vanished behind them, for a world of the past.

And there. What they have in Portland blurs into background noise.

The property. The land. It's flat, empty. But full of sharp-cornered houses, all whitish-gray and all the same. Lined up and nice, they stand divided by a paved road that runs smooth and straight, easing into a bend at the end of Twenty-Second Terrace to show more homes of the same build, the same style, the same size.

Palmblad Meadows.

Where these solid wooden steps lead up to a robin's-egg blue door, the teen as a child stood to decorate the front porch with fake spiderwebs under the real spiderwebs each Halloween.

Where this shiny Dodge Ram is parked there, the mound at the end of the gravel driveway the child called Zaji Mountain had stood proudly in front of two looming, swaying trees that stood like pillars holding up the sky.

Where those two houses stand behind perfect too-green lawns, the sisters jumped on their trampoline, danced in grasses that needed to be mown, swung on the tire swing, and picked berries— all within an hour.

Where that small window peers out from under a slate-gray roof, the child sat on her fuzzy bedroom rug every night and stretched in her left, right, and middle splits, pressing down until she sat flat in each one.

Where that woman is emerging from her tan-colored garage in tan-colored heels, the mother chopped wood at an ancient tree stump.

Where that boy stands on the sidewalk texting on his phone, the sisters stood in front of the Christmas tree making sure each other's hair looked nice enough before leaving to see *The Nutcracker* with their mother.

I could go on.

The three stare and think. It isn't the others' faults, the new people who walk on memories. They don't know about putting plastic wrap and tape on a broken window or buying wood for the fireplace when a heater isn't always enough. They don't know about the howl of the wind on fall and winter nights that makes an old home creak or the feeling of a constant presence from hidden wild creatures. They are making homes from houses on a property that used to be someone else's, a property that was held on to for as long as possible but was ultimately, finally, given away. They are making homes on a property that is not theirs, and the three, like them, adjust.

BUT, IN A WAY, a part of the house remains. There is a solidness of roots underfoot where these new homes stand, deeper than the foundations and churning with feelings, words, and hearts.

IT LIVES ON, AND it is not going anywhere.

Child

THE PORTLAND STATE CAMPUS is different in the midday light. Unlike the abrasive classroom lights, or the pink late-afternoon light of downtown glowing on the dwindling number of students, this bright Friday makes things shine and feel like they are in bustling motion. All the nights of sleepy dry-eyed doodling on lined paper while my mom studied before she graduated, all the long train rides with her to and from the college when my sister had the car, seem like they were at a different PSU and it was a different us.

When we step outside and into the welcome unseasonal warmth of April's sun, excitement sets in. Bookstores are where worlds happen.

The printer's desk is downstairs, and we pass textbooks with prices like $150, a crime that nearly makes me walk out. I push away the familiar temptation to ask my mom to talk for me, making myself say to the stranger at the desk that I ordered five books via email, saying that my name is *Za–ji, yes, that's right, it definitely is a unique name, ha!* He clicks a few times on the computer, then reaches down to a place underneath the desk.

There are other books here: perfect bound, hardcover, and

spiral bound; pages in varying shades of white and wrapped in plastic. The covers are in all kinds of shades, patterns, and colors, with ambiguous titles like *White Autumn* and *The Days I Claimed*. I want to unwrap and feel and smell them all.

My heart jumps: there's a cover in mostly blues and greens in a perfect stack of five. I wait for the man to spot them and then suddenly they are in front of me.

My word magic: *Journey into ArJarelia*. The cover has printed exactly right, just as it looked on the computer at home. My hand-drawn and photoshopped art of three kids standing in front of a forest and facing the unknown, ready for an adventure.

I take the top copy and turn it over in my hands, flipping through the pages to make certain the text is printed correctly but also to secretly inhale the scent of freshly printed ink. It is a sensory delight of handwritten to typed to printed. Kids stumbling into a world of pirates, gatekeepers, and endless oceans, letters scribbled under a purple hanging lamp for hours at a time, somehow transformed into *a real book*. Inside I am a melting puddle of *I seriously just did this*, but what comes out is "These look great" and a polite smile.

My mom's smile is like the sun on my back.

The I-seriously-just-did-this feeling remains as we go to eat at Chipotle, me flipping through the pages multiple times and that mysterious all-knowing mother smile on my mom's face. It's one of the rare times I am able to express and articulate my feelings. What a day.

I hold one of the copies up in front of me. Meaning to say, *my book* with reverence and awe, I slip and say, "My *child*."

My mom laughs with me. "A lot of authors call their books their children."

"Really?" I'm puzzled. "That's … weird."

She does that nod that shows she's certain about something and knows things. "Yup. So you're right on track with that. This is just the beginning."

My laugh is soft now as I shake my head. But my mom, with her mysterious all-knowing mother smile, seems to be convinced. Of something.

Dusk Creatures II

THEY ARE FERAL, SLOWLY encroaching and claiming new terri-
tories, howling to no one now but each other, singing no one to
sleep now but themselves, their young, and the neighboring cats
and bats, on the edge of a land that becomes more and more
overgrown, more and more unkempt, more and more wild like
them.

About the Author

ZAJI COX HAS BEEN a storyteller since she started reading at age three. She wrote her first short story at nine years old, followed by self-publishing a fantasy adventure novel at thirteen. Her high school senior project became another book in 2016. She was the winner in the poetry category of Submission PDX's reading series in 2020, and she has performed at the PDX Poetry Festival, Survival of the Feminist reading series, Corporeal Writing's LOOP, the 50th annual Northwest Folklife Festival, and XRAY FM's Amplify Women teach-in for International Women's Day. She holds a bachelor's degree in English from Portland State. Her writing can be found in *Pathos Literary Magazine, Entropy, The Portland Metrozine, Cultural Daily, CARE Covid Art REsource,* the print anthology *2020: The Year of the Asterisk* (University of Hell Press), and others. She lives in Portland, Oregon.

Acknowledgments

I ABSOLUTELY MUST EXPRESS thanks to my publisher, Laura Stanfill, for believing in me and my work. Your open mind, enthusiasm, and patience through the entire process of making this book into a physical thing has been a highlight in my writing life. I am so glad for that garden party.

Thank you to those willing to read this book early on, and to the amazing individuals at Forest Avenue Press for helping bring it to life. From the smallest edits to the most eye-catching elements of the cover design, I could not have imagined it turning out this way—and I couldn't be happier.

Gratitude must be extended toward the Corporeal Writing family and those I have come to know through Corporeal Writing workshops. I wouldn't be the writer I am without all the support, feedback, guidance, and friendship these past years I have been involved. It's a very long list of people, but if you think you're part of it, then you are.

Thank you to Lidia Yuknavitch and Jen Pastiloff—I know you've got me.

And, of course, thank you to my family. This book would not exist without you all.

PLUMS
FOR
MONTHS

READERS'
GUIDE

Book Club Questions

1. Are Zaji's chapters micro essays? Or prose poems? Or both? Find a few chapters with different formatting and consider why each breaks the established design pattern.

2. Consider the title of the memoir. What does Plums for Months evoke for you? How does the title connect to the idea of abundance, especially when juxtaposed with descriptions of growing up in a low-income household?

3. Are there any places from your childhood that still exist—an apartment building? A park? A movie theater? A school? A library? Choose one and share some sensory memories of that place. If you get stuck, start describing what you remember (the kitchen, the sticky movie-theater aisle, the bright carpet in the children's section of the library). Then think about how you felt in that place. How those smells, colors, and sounds impacted you as a child.

4. What are some other memoirs you can think of that focus on childhood and becoming? How about any memoirs that focus on joy instead of trauma?

5. Were you surprised when Zaji's teacher suggests she has autism? Why or why not? If you are autistic and feel comfortable sharing, are there any experiences on the page that reminded you of your childhood? What about differences?

6. Consider the chapter "What We Are," about race and identity. In what other chapters does the author write about race? If you were to write a paragraph about your identity, what might it say?

7. There are cats on the front cover of the memoir and their tiny faces peek out from section breaks. Why are animals so important to Zaji? Would it surprise you to know she works with animals as an adult?

8. Words—writing, reading, and the Scholastic Book Fair—make Zaji feel at home and grounded in her identity. What specific places or routines offer the author that same kind of comfort?